11+ Maths

For **GL** Assessment

This CGP Practice Book is perfect for children aged 7-8 —
it's a fantastic way to start building the skills they'll need for the GL 11+.

It starts with accessible questions to help them get to grips with the basics,
one topic at a time. Once they're happy with those, there's a selection of mixed-topic
Assessment Tests to introduce them to the style of the real 11+ papers.

We've also included full answers in a pull-out booklet, so marking is a piece of cake!

How to access your free Online Edition

This book includes a free Online Edition to read on your PC, Mac or tablet.
You'll just need to go to **cgpbooks.co.uk/extras** and enter this code:

0436 8093 0158 7584

By the way, this code only works for one person. If somebody else has used
this book before you, they might have already claimed the Online Edition.

Practice Book – Ages 7-8

with Assessment Tests

How to use this Practice Book

This book is divided into two parts — themed question practice and assessment tests.
There are answers and detailed explanations in the pull-out section at the end of the book.

Themed question practice

- Each page contains practice questions divided by topic. Use these pages to work out your child's strengths and the areas they find tricky. The questions get harder down each page.

- Your child can use the smiley face tick boxes to evaluate how confident they feel with each topic.

Assessment tests

- The second half of the book contains six assessment tests, each with a mix of question types from the first half of the book. They take a similar form to the real test.

- You can print off multiple-choice answer sheets from cgpbooks.co.uk/11plus/answer-sheets, so your child can practise taking the tests as if they're sitting the real thing.

- Use the printable answer sheets if you want your child to do each test more than once.

- If you want to give your child timed practice, give them a time limit of 30 minutes for each test, and ask them to work as quickly and carefully as they can.

- Your child should aim for a mark of around 85% (21 questions correct) in each test. If they score less than this, use their results to work out the areas they need more practice on.

- If they haven't managed to finish the test in time, they need to work on increasing their speed, whereas if they have made a lot of mistakes, they need to work more carefully.

- Keep track of your child's scores using the progress chart on the inside back cover of the book.

Published by CGP

Editors:
Luke Antieul, Joe Brazier, David Broadbent, Sharon Keeley-Holden, Megan Tyler, Sarah Williams

Contributors:
Stephanie Burton, Sumyya Hassan, Dan Heaney, Julie Hunt

With thanks to Rachel Murray and Glenn Rogers for the proofreading.

ISBN: 978 1 78908 156 5
Printed by Elanders Ltd, Newcastle upon Tyne
Clipart from Corel®

Based on the classic CGP style created by Richard Parsons.

Contents

Tick off the check box for each topic as you go along.

Place Value

Circle the biggest number in each row.

1. 45   30   60   65   15
2. 56   81   45   61   89
3. 29   76   52   37   73
4. 765   667   566   776   577
5. 325   231   233   322   323

/ 5

Write down each number below in digits.

6.   Six hundred and seventy-five   Answer: _____

7.   Seven hundred and twenty-six   Answer: _____

8.   Nine hundred and eighty-nine   Answer: _____

9.   Two hundred and twelve   Answer: _____

10. Four hundred and two   Answer: _____

/ 5

What number is the arrow pointing to on each of these number lines?

11. ↓ (between 16 and 18, on 17)
    10   12   14   16   18   20   Answer: _____

12. ↓ (around 30)
    0   20   40   60   80   100   Answer: _____

13. ↓ (around 12)
    0   10   20   Answer: _____

14. ↓ (around 20)
    0   25   50   Answer: _____

15. ↓ (around 175)
    100   150   200   Answer: _____

/ 5

Place Value

16. Write down the number which completes this sentence:

    542 has 5 hundreds, _____ tens and 2 units.

17. Circle the heaviest weight.

    345 g   312 g   349 g   394 g   321 g   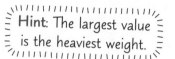 Hint: The largest value is the heaviest weight.

18. There are 613 children at Sol's school. Write the number 613 in words.

    Answer: _____

19. Circle the letter of the arrow which is pointing at 215.

    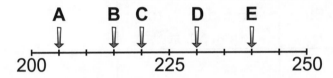

20. What is the smallest number you can make
    when you rearrange the digits in 582?   Answer: _____

21. Five children in Class 3H ran in a fun run.
    The distances they ran were put into this table.
    Circle the name of the person who ran the
    shortest distance.

    Sam   Joe   Ami   Ben   Chi

Sam	121 m
Joe	212 m
Ami	122 m
Ben	112 m
Chi	201 m

22. Circle the number which is closest to 200.
    196   212   214   206   191

23. Here are the distances between London and three towns in Britain.

    234 km   252 km   245 km

    Write down these distances in order from the largest to the smallest.

    Answer: _____   / 8

                Section One — Number Knowledge

Rounding Up and Down

Round the following numbers to the nearest 10.

1. 49   Answer: _____

2. 54   Answer: _____

3. 62   Answer: _____

4. 75   Answer: _____

5. 98   Answer: _____

/ 5

Complete the table so it shows each number rounded to the nearest 10 and 100.

	Number	Rounded to the nearest 10	Rounded to the nearest 100
6.	348	350	
7.	264		300
8.	239		200
9.	876	880	
10.	651	650	

/ 5

Round the following amounts to the nearest £1.

11. £1.34   Answer: £ _____

12. £2.95   Answer: £ _____

13. £3.49   Answer: £ _____

14. £7.82   Answer: £ _____

15. £4.47   Answer: £ _____

/ 5

Rounding Up and Down

16. A zookeeper counted 921 stick insects.
    Round the number of stick insects to the nearest 10.

    Answer: _____

17. A window is 87 cm tall. What is this
    height rounded to the nearest 10 cm?   Answer: _____ cm

18. Sally has 452 marbles. How many marbles does she
    have to the nearest 100? Circle the correct answer.

    A 400   **B** 450   **C** 500   **D** 460   **E** 1000

19. Hamish ran 742 m in a race.
    What is this distance to the nearest 100 m?   Answer: _____ m

20. A box contains 345 lollipops.
    What is 345 rounded to the nearest 10?

    Answer: _____

21. Terry has 147 garden gnomes in his garden.
    How many gnomes does he have to the nearest 100?

    Answer: _____

22. Which of these numbers is 347 rounded to the nearest 10?
    Circle the correct answer.

    A 300   **B** 400   **C** 340   **D** 350   **E** 345

23. The Pearson family travels 157 km to get to the beach.
    How far is this distance to the nearest 100 km?

    Answer: _____ km

24. Jackie has £6.98. What is this amount to the nearest 10p?
    Circle the correct answer.

    A £6.90   **C** £6.50   **E** £10.00

    B £7.00   **D** £6.00

/ 9

Number Knowledge

Circle the even number in each row.

1.   3   5   6   7   9

2.   34   39   45   73   99

3.   321   435   721   452   879

4.   45   671   39   375   272

5.   23   46   543   237   985

/ 5

| 21 | 15 | 32 | 12 | 81 |

Which of the numbers in the box is:

Hint: Use your times tables to help you with these questions.

6.   a multiple of 6?   Answer: _____

7.   a multiple of 5?   Answer: _____

8.   a multiple of 9?   Answer: _____

9.   a multiple of 8?   Answer: _____

10. a multiple of 7?   Answer: _____

/ 5

Circle 'True' or 'False' for each of these statements.

11. All whole numbers ending in 4 are multiples of 2.   True / False

12. All whole numbers ending in 3 are multiples of 3.   True / False

13. All whole numbers ending in 2, 4, 6, 7 and 0 are even.   True / False

14. Adding together two odd numbers gives an odd number.   True / False

15. Write down the even numbers between 47 and 53.

     Answer: _____

/ 5

Number Knowledge

16. What is the last odd number before 41?   Answer: _____

17. How many even numbers smaller than 21 are there in this circle?

    Answer: _____

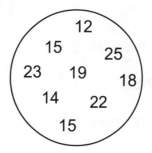

18. Circle the statement which is true.

A	9 < 7	**C**	4 > 6	**E**	3 > 13
B	10 > 4	**D**	12 < 8		

    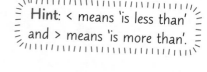
    Hint: < means 'is less than' and > means 'is more than'.

19. Circle the number which should be put in the shaded section of the Venn diagram.

    16   20   24   28   30

    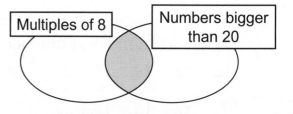

    Hint: The number in the shaded section has to be bigger than 20 and a multiple of 8.

20. Circle the statement which is true.

    A All multiples of 4 end in 4.

    B All multiples of 3 are even numbers.

    C All multiples of 5 end in 0.

    D All multiples of 4 are even numbers.

    E All multiples of 7 end in 5.

21. Look at the sorting diagram on the right. Circle the number that is in the wrong place.

	odd	even
multiple of 5	25 45	10
not a multiple of 5	18	24

22. Each page in a photo album holds 4 photos. Circle the person who has enough photos to fill exactly 4 pages of the album.

    A Joe has 12 photos.

    B Mo has 8 photos.

    C Sue has 16 photos.

    D Tom has 24 photos.

    E Azhar has 20 photos.

/ 7

Section One — Number Knowledge

Number Sequences

Write down the missing number in each of the sequences below.

1. Add 4 each time: 14   18   22   26   _____

2. Subtract 2 each time: 20   18   16   14   _____

3. Add 5 each time: 12   _____   22   27   32

4. Subtract 6 each time: 29   23   17   _____   5

5. Add 8 each time: _____   25   33   41   49

/ 5

Write down the next number in each of the sequences below.

6. 22, 24, 26, 28   Answer: _____

7. 12, 15, 18, 21   Answer: _____

8. 30, 25, 20, 15   Answer: _____

9. 21, 17, 13, 9   Answer: _____

10. 1, 7, 13, 19   Answer: _____

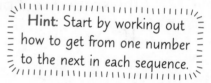

Hint: Start by working out how to get from one number to the next in each sequence.

/ 5

Hint: Work out the 6th number of the sequence and use it to find the 7th number.

Write the **7th** number of each sequence in the space provided:

	1st Number	2nd Number	3rd Number	4th Number	5th Number	6th Number	7th Number
11.	3	5	7	9	11		....
12.	20	17	14	11	8		....
13.	7	12	17	22	27		....
14.	33	29	25	21	17		....
15.	72	63	54	45	36		....

/ 5

Number Sequences

16. Nicky counts on from 3 in equal steps to make a sequence.
    She missed out the 3rd number in the sequence.
    Write down the missing number.

    3,   9,   _____,   21,   27

17. Cynthia writes a sequence starting with 15. Her rule is 'subtract 3'.
    What is the 3rd number in her sequence?

    Answer: _____

18. Vikram counted on from 1 in steps of 4.
    Which of these numbers will be in his sequence? Circle the correct answer.

    12   10   15   8   17

19. Sally starts a sequence with the number 9. She uses the rule 'add 9'
    to make the sequence. Circle the 3rd number in the sequence.

    27   30   38   45   55

20. Jamil counts backwards from 52 in steps of 10.
    What is the 5th number in his sequence?   Answer: _____

21. Ben counts on in equal steps of 5 to make a sequence. The 5th number in his
    sequence was 29. What number did Ben start at? Circle the correct answer.

    9   5   8   6   7

22. Luis is making a sequence of patterns
    with matchsticks. How many
    matchsticks will there be in the next
    pattern of the sequence?

    Answer: _____

    Pattern 1

    Pattern 2

    Pattern 3

    Hint: Think of the number of matches in each pattern as numbers in a sequence.

23. Estelle is counting backwards from 20. She counts in steps of 7.
    What is the last number that she will count before 0?
    Circle the correct answer.

    2   4   8   6   5

/ 8

Section One — Number Knowledge

Fractions

A fraction of each of these shapes is shaded. Write down the letter of the shape that matches each fraction.

1. $\frac{1}{2}$ Answer: _____

2. $\frac{3}{4}$ Answer: _____

3. $\frac{1}{8}$ Answer: _____

4. $\frac{1}{4}$ Answer: _____

5. $\frac{1}{10}$ Answer: _____

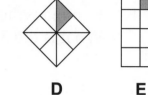

A   **B**

C   **D**   **E**

/ 5

Write down the answer to these fraction calculations.

6. $\frac{1}{2}$ of 8   Answer: _____

7. $\frac{1}{3}$ of 12   Answer: _____

8. $\frac{1}{3}$ of 9   Answer: _____

9. $\frac{1}{5}$ of 15   Answer: _____

10. $\frac{1}{4}$ of 20   Answer: _____

/ 5

Circle the largest fraction in each row.

11. $\frac{4}{6}$ $\frac{1}{6}$ $\frac{3}{6}$

12. $\frac{4}{8}$ $\frac{7}{8}$ $\frac{6}{8}$

13. $\frac{6}{10}$ $\frac{4}{10}$ $\frac{8}{10}$

> **Hint**: When fractions have the same bottom number (denominator), you can find the biggest fraction by comparing the top numbers (numerators).

Circle the largest amount in each pair given below.

14. $\frac{1}{4}$ of 16   or   3

15. $\frac{1}{5}$ of 5   or   2

Write down the answer to these fraction calculations.

16. $\frac{2}{7} + \frac{3}{7}$ Answer: _____

17. $\frac{4}{5} - \frac{2}{5}$ Answer: _____

/ 7

Fractions

18. Cathy eats $^1/_5$ of a cake.
    What fraction of the cake is left?

    Answer: _____

19. 20 children went on a bus. $^1/_4$ of the children were boys
    and the rest were girls. How many boys were there?

    Answer: _____

20. Harry eats $^1/_5$ of a chocolate bar. The bar is made up of
    15 squares in total. How many squares did Harry eat?

    Answer: _____

21. William buys a cinema ticket at half price. If the full
    price of a ticket is £4.80, how much did William pay?

    Answer: £ _____

22. Sam had 21p in his pocket. He spent some of this
    money, but he kept $^1/_3$ of it. How much did he keep?

    Answer: _____ p

23. Which arrow is pointing at $^5/_6$?

    A   B   C   D   E

    Answer: _____

    0   1

24. Circle the shape which
    is $^5/_8$ shaded.

    A   B   C   D   E

25. $^1/_2$ of the square on the right is shaded. Which of these
    squares has an equal amount shaded? Circle your answer.

    A   B   C   D   E

    / 8

Addition

Write down the answer to each calculation.

1. 25 + 3   Answer: _____

Hint: Splitting a number into tens and units often makes it easier to add on.

2. 62 + 12   Answer: _____

3. 43 + 27   Answer: _____

4. 23 + 58   Answer: _____

/ 4

5. Add 18 and 22.   Answer: _____

6. What is one hundred plus seven?   Answer: _____

7. What is the sum of 15p and 19p?   Answer: _____ p

8. What is the sum of 20, 22 and 9?   Answer: _____

/ 4

Use the price list to work out how much each person spends.

Pencil	15p
Rubber	20p
Ruler	50p
Pen	68p

9. Jack buys a pencil and a ruler.   Answer: _____ p

10. Jemma buys a pen and a pencil.   Answer: _____ p

11. Ahmed buys a pencil, a rubber and a ruler.   Answer: _____ p

12. Harry buys a pen and two pencils.   Answer: _____ p

/ 4

13. Sam is 28 years old.
    How old will he be in 3 years?   Answer: _____

14. There are 16 people on a bus. 27 more people get on the bus.
    How many people are on the bus now?   Answer: _____

15. The table shows how much money Ella
    and her friends have raised for charity.
    How much money did they raise altogether?

Ella	£2
John	£5
Samantha	£8
Dee	£6

    Answer: £ _____

/ 3

Addition

16. Kim's pet dog eats 65 g of food in the morning. He eats the same amount of food in the evening. How much food does he eat in one day?

    Answer: _____ g

17. Amy buys a coat for £39 and some shoes for £25. How much does she spend altogether? Circle the correct answer.

    A £64   **C** £14   **E** £65

    B £46   **D** £54

18. Helen goes to the seaside. The seaside is 140 miles from her house. What is the total number of miles she travels to get there and back?

    Answer: _____ miles

19. The table shows the weight of fruit in a bowl. What is the total weight of the fruit? Circle the correct answer.

Apples	200 g
Pears	150 g
Oranges	350 g
Bananas	300 g

    A 800 g   **C** 950 g   **E** 1100 g

    B 750 g   **D** 1000 g

20. Which of these additions equals 386? Circle the correct answer.

    A 300 + 80   **C** 300 + 186   **E** 200 + 156

    B 100 + 136   **D** 200 + 186

21. Rashid has two jars of marbles.
    There are 262 marbles in one jar and 88 in the other.
    How many marbles does Rashid have altogether?   Answer: _____

22. The table shows the number of children in Years 3 and 4. How many children are in Years 3 and 4 in total? Circle the correct answer.

Year 3	107
Year 4	129

    A 136   **C** 236   **E** 238

    B 234   **D** 134

Section Two — Working with Numbers

Subtraction

Write down the answer to each calculation.

1. 19 – 6　　　　　　Answer: _____

2. 27 – 15　　　　　　Answer: _____

3. 158 – 20　　　　　Answer: _____

4. 24 – 11　　　　　　Answer: _____

5. 154 – 33　　　　　Answer: _____

 / 5

6. What is 9 take away 2?　　　　　　Answer: _____

7. What is the difference between 48 and 5?　Answer: _____

8. What number is 10 less than 74?　　Answer: _____

9. What is 29 minus 18?　　　　　　Answer: _____

10. What number is 250 fewer than 380?　Answer: _____

 / 5

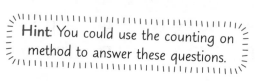

Hint: You could use the counting on method to answer these questions.

11. Pei Ling spends 22p. How much change will she get from £1?

    Answer: _____ p

12. Mahendra spends 70p. How much change will he get from £2?

    Answer: £ _____

13. Jamie spends £2.40. How much change will he get from £5?

    Answer: £ _____

14. Bianca spends £7.60. How much change will she get from £10?

    Answer: £ _____

15. Angus spends £1.80. How much change will he get from £2?

    Answer: _____ p

/ 5

Subtraction

16. Bruno grows two plants. One plant is 6 cm tall and the other is 15 cm tall. What is the difference in height between the two plants?

    Answer: _____ cm

17. Emma wants to buy a game which costs £42. Emma has saved £15. How much more money does she need to save to buy the game?

    Answer: £ _____

18. What is 140 – 78?

    Answer: _____

19. Class 3H are saving book tokens. They need 400 altogether and so far they have saved 220. How many more tokens do they need?
    Circle the correct answer.

    A 190 **B** 180 **C** 80 **D** 210 **E** 620

20. Jill has a 64 cm long piece of wood. She cuts it into two pieces. One piece is 36 cm long. How long is the other piece?

    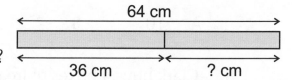

    Answer: _____ cm

21. Look at these numbers:

    701   610   800   798

    Circle the pair of numbers which have a difference of 99.

    A 701 and 610   **C** 701 and 798   **E** 610 and 798
    B 701 and 800   **D** 610 and 800

22. 297 – 130 = ☐

    Circle the missing number in this calculation.

    A 165 **B** 187 **C** 155 **D** 167 **E** 176

23. Viktor had 495 beads. He gave 173 of them to Ashley. How many beads does Viktor have left? Circle the correct answer.

    A 334 **B** 327 **C** 322 **D** 317 **E** 312

/ 8

Section Two — Working with Numbers

Multiplying and Dividing by 10 and 100

Fill in the gaps to complete the calculations below.

1. 10 × 7 = _____

2. 80 ÷ 10 = _____

3. _____ × 10 = 40

4. 100 × 9 = _____

5. 500 ÷ 100 = _____

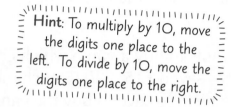

Hint: To multiply by 10, move the digits one place to the left. To divide by 10, move the digits one place to the right.

/ 5

6. How many lots of 10p are in £1?   Answer: _____

7. Jamal is using a 'multiply by 10' machine. He puts a number into the machine and it comes out as 70. Circle the number that Jamal put into the machine.

? ⟶ × 10 ⟶ 70

   A 10   **B** 7   **C** 5   **D** 8   **E** 6

8. Clark buys 4 boxes of treats for his dog. There are 100 treats in a box. How many treats does he buy altogether?   Answer: _____

9. ☐ ÷ 10 = 15

   Circle the missing number in this calculation.

   A 100   **B** 15   **C** 1500   **D** 250   **E** 150

10. 10 tickets to watch Grizebridge Town cost £90. How much does 1 ticket cost?   Answer: £ _____

11. Year 3 have collected 600 stamps for charity. They put the stamps into bags that each contain 100 stamps. How many bags do they use?   Answer: _____

12. Hattie's horse eats 12 sugar lumps each week. How many sugar lumps will her horse eat in 10 weeks?

    Answer: _____

/ 7

Section Two — Working with Numbers

Multiplication

Fill in the gaps to complete the calculations below.

1. $6 \times 2 = $ _____

2. $4 \times 5 = $ _____

3. $3 \times 9 = $ _____

4. _____ $\times 6 = 30$

5. $8 \times$ _____ $= 16$

/ 5

Hint: The product of
6 and 4 means 6×4.

Work out the answer to these questions.

6. What is the product of 6 and 4?   Answer: _____

7. What is 7 multiplied by 3?   Answer: _____

8. What are 5 lots of 8?   Answer: _____

9. What is 9 multiplied by 6?   Answer: _____

/ 5

10. How many sevens make thirty-five?   Answer: _____

Look at the animals below:

Spider   Cat   Ladybird   Blackbird
8 legs   4 legs   6 legs   2 legs

Use the information about the animals to answer these questions.

11. How many legs do 4 cats have?   Answer: _____

12. How many legs do 9 blackbirds have?   Answer: _____

13. How many legs do 5 spiders have?   Answer: _____

14. How many legs do 7 ladybirds have?   Answer: _____

/ 5

15. How many legs do 8 spiders have?   Answer: _____

Multiplication

16. ☐ × 6 = 18

What is the missing number in this calculation? Circle the correct answer.

A 6   **B** 9   **C** 2   **D** 4   **E** 3

17. A car has four wheels. How many wheels do seven cars have?

Answer: _____

18. Suresh has eight 5p coins.   How much
money does he have altogether?   Answer: _____ p

19. Juliet buys 6 boxes of eggs.
Each box contains 6 eggs.
How many eggs does she buy altogether?   Answer: _____

20. How many days are there in 3 weeks?   Answer: _____

Hint: There are 7 days in a week.

21. There are 8 tables in Roman's classroom.
There are 7 chairs around each table.
How many chairs are there in total?   Answer: _____

22. Pencils cost 9p each.
How much do 20 pencils cost?   Answer: £ _____

23. Martha bought a model plane for £15.
She sells it for seven times its original price.
How much does she sell it for?
Circle the correct answer.

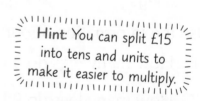

Hint: You can split £15 into tens and units to make it easier to multiply.

A £150   **B** £90   **C** £105   **D** £135   **E** £85

24. What is the product of 18 and 8? Circle the correct answer.

A 104   **B** 26   **C** 96   **D** 164   **E** 144

/ 9

Division

Fill in the gaps to complete the calculations below.

1. $12 \div 2 =$ _____

2. $20 \div 5 =$ _____

3. $24 \div 6 =$ _____

4. _____ $\div 8 = 4$

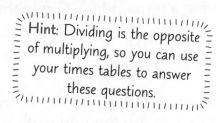
Hint: Dividing is the opposite of multiplying, so you can use your times tables to answer these questions.

/ 4

Work out the answer to these questions.

5. What is 25 divided by 5?   Answer: _____

6. How many threes are there in 27?   Answer: _____

7. How many lots of 7 are there in 63?   Answer: _____

8. What is 48 divided by 6?   Answer: _____

/ 4

Write down the remainder in each calculation.

9. $15 \div 2$ Answer: 7 remainder _____

10. $27 \div 4$ Answer: 6 remainder _____

11. $32 \div 3$ Answer: 10 remainder _____

12. $47 \div 6$ Answer: 7 remainder _____

/ 4

13. Sharon and Gary have 18 stickers. They share them
     equally. How many stickers do they each get?   Answer: _____

14. 25 children are playing football. There are 5 children in each team.
     How many teams are there? Circle the correct answer.

     A 4   **B** 1   **C** 5   **D** 3   **E** 7

15. Class 3H go camping. 5 children sleep in
     each tent. There are 35 children in the class.
     How many tents do they need?   Answer: _____

/ 3

Division

16. Which of these numbers can be divided by three
    without giving a remainder? Circle the correct answer.

    A 28 **B** 31 **C** 33 **D** 23 **E** 19

17. Anne's class are planting carrots. They plant 72 carrots in 8 rows.
    How many carrots are there in each row?

    Answer: _____

18. Circle the calculation below which is incorrect.

    A $32 \div 4 = 8$ **C** $30 \div 3 = 10$ **E** $54 \div 6 = 9$

    B $40 \div 8 = 5$ **D** $48 \div 8 = 7$

19. What is 63 divided by 9? Circle the correct answer.

    A 4 **B** 7 **C** 8 **D** 5 **E** 6

20. Three friends share 60p equally.
    How much money does each friend get?

    Answer: _____ p

    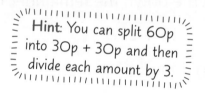
    Hint: You can split 60p into 30p + 30p and then divide each amount by 3.

21. Jane has 90p in 5p coins. How many 5p
    coins does she have? Circle the correct answer.

    A 20 **B** 12 **C** 18 **D** 15 **E** 25

22. $40 \div 9 = \boxed{}$ remainder $\boxed{}$

    Which of these numbers should be added to both boxes in this calculation?
    Circle the correct answer.

    A 4 **B** 2 **C** 8 **D** 6 **E** 9

23. Kaye is baking 32 muffins. Each baking tray holds
    6 muffins. How many baking trays does she need?

    Answer: _____

    / 8

Section Two — Working with Numbers

Word Problems

1. Charlie has 6 rabbits. Each rabbit eats 7 carrots a day.
   How many carrots do they eat in total each day?   Answer: _____

2. Tahsin buys a chocolate bar for 35p. She pays with a one pound coin.
   How much change does she get? Circle the correct answer.

   A   65p   **B**   55p   **C**   75p   **D**   85p   **E**   60p

3. Sarah thinks of a number and multiplies it by ten.
   The answer is 80. What was Sarah's number?   Answer: _____

4. William goes to a farm to buy some eggs.
   He buys 6 duck eggs. How much does he spend?
   Circle the correct answer.

   Eggs for sale
   duck eggs   9p each
   chicken eggs 8p each

   A   60p   **B**   54p   **C**   48p   **D**   15p   **E**   9p

5. Zani buys a dress in a half-price sale. She pays £16.
   How much was the dress before the sale?   Answer: £ _____

6. Mohammed thinks of a number and takes away 15.
   The answer is 38. What was Mohammed's number?   Answer: _____

7. Mina goes to the funfair. She goes on the ghost train twice,
   the bumper cars twice and the helter-skelter once.
   How much money does she spend?
   Circle the correct answer.

   Funfair Rides
   helter-skelter 50p
   bumper cars £1
   ghost train 50p

   A   £3   **C**   £2   **E**   £4

   B   £2.50   **D**   £3.50

8. Sanjay made eight pies. He sold them for 20p each.
   How much money did he get?   Answer: £ _____

9. Andre bought a rubber for 35p, a pencil for 25p and a sharpener for 33p.
   How much money did he spend altogether? Circle the correct answer.

   A   99p   **B**   93p   **C**   83p   **D**   98p   **E**   92p   / 9

Word Problems

10. Nahid builds a tower using blocks. His tower is 32 cm high. Each block is 4 cm tall. How many blocks are in the tower? Circle the correct answer.

    A 9   **B** 10   **C** 6   **D** 4   **E** 8

    4 cm
    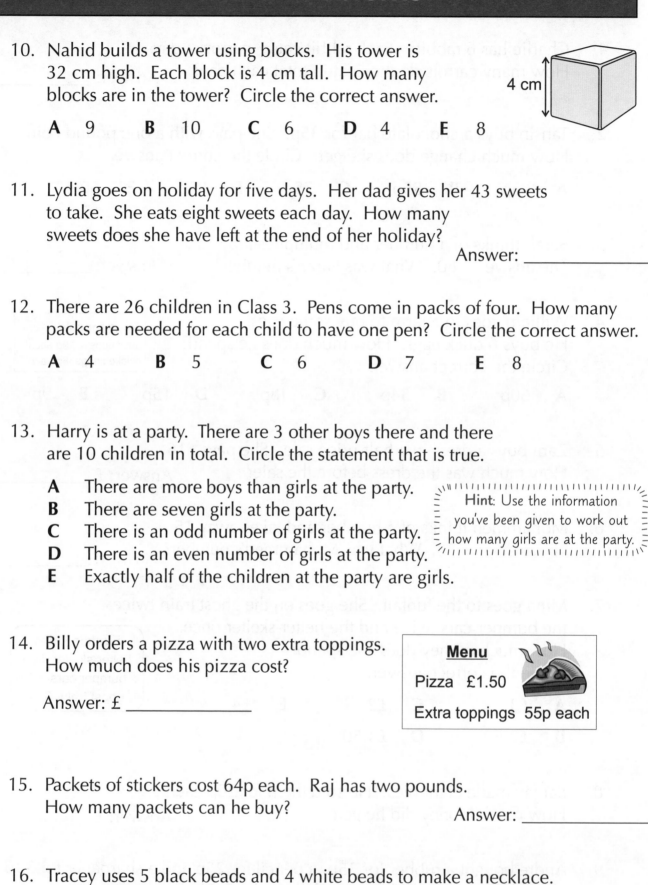

11. Lydia goes on holiday for five days. Her dad gives her 43 sweets to take. She eats eight sweets each day. How many sweets does she have left at the end of her holiday?

    Answer: _____

12. There are 26 children in Class 3. Pens come in packs of four. How many packs are needed for each child to have one pen? Circle the correct answer.

    A 4   **B** 5   **C** 6   **D** 7   **E** 8

13. Harry is at a party. There are 3 other boys there and there are 10 children in total. Circle the statement that is true.

    A   There are more boys than girls at the party.
    B   There are seven girls at the party.
    C   There is an odd number of girls at the party.
    D   There is an even number of girls at the party.
    E   Exactly half of the children at the party are girls.

    Hint: Use the information you've been given to work out how many girls are at the party.

14. Billy orders a pizza with two extra toppings. How much does his pizza cost?

    Answer: £ _____

    Menu
    Pizza   £1.50
    Extra toppings   55p each

15. Packets of stickers cost 64p each. Raj has two pounds. How many packets can he buy?

    Answer: _____

16. Tracey uses 5 black beads and 4 white beads to make a necklace. The black beads are 7 cm long and the white beads are 3 cm long. How long is her necklace?

    Answer: _____ cm

    / 7

Section Three — Word Problems

Data Tables

Mrs Burton has a bag of sweets. She records the number and colour of the sweets in the table below.

1. How many green jelly bears has she got?

   Answer: _____

2. How many red jelly snakes has she got?

   Answer: _____

Sweet	Green	Red
Jelly bears	3	?
Jelly snakes	4	7
Total	?	9

3. How many green sweets has she got in total?   Answer: _____

4. How many red jelly bears has she got?   Answer: _____

/ 4

5. The table shows the length of five people's legs.

Name	Bernard	Shaznay	Tony	Nathaniel	Beth
Length of leg (cm)	50	53	51	48	52

Who has the longest legs?   Answer: _____

6. Siobhan used a table to record the temperature of some cities in the UK.

London	Manchester	Cardiff	Edinburgh	Belfast
12 °C	10 °C	11 °C	7 °C	9 °C

How much warmer was Manchester than Edinburgh?
Circle the correct answer.

A   1 °C   **B**   2 °C   **C**   3 °C   **D**   4 °C   **E**   5 °C

7. 10 children went swimming. The table shows how many lengths they swam. How many children swam 15 lengths?

   Answer: _____

Number of lengths	Number of children
5	4
10	5
15	?

8. Ian and Mark collect snails. They recorded the number of snails they have in the table. How many snails have they collected in total?

	Big snails	Little snails
Ian	12	6
Mark	9	17

Answer: _____

/ 4

Displaying Data

Arthur is collecting objects at a beach. He makes the bar chart below to show the number of each object he collects.

1. How many fossils did he collect?

   Answer: _____

2. How many shark teeth did he collect?

   Answer: _____

3. Which object did he collect six of?

   Answer: _____

4. Which object did he collect fewest of?

   Answer: _____

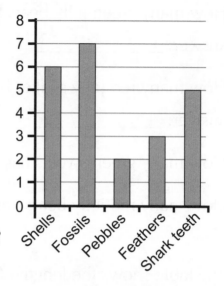

/ 4

5. Class 3J do a times tables test every Friday. Their teacher made a pictogram to show the number of children that scored full marks each week. How many children scored full marks in Week 3?

   Answer: _____

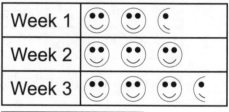

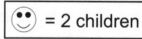 = 2 children

Hint: Work out how many children are shown by half a symbol.

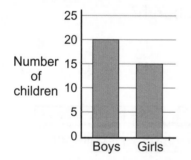

6. The bar chart shows the number of boys and girls in John's class. How many children are in John's class?

   Answer: _____

7. Emily asked her friends how many soft toys they have. She made a pictogram of the results. How many more soft toys does George have than Seren? Circle the correct answer.

   A 5   D 9

   B 6   E 12

   C 8

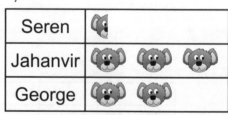

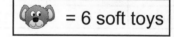 = 6 soft toys

/ 3

Displaying Data

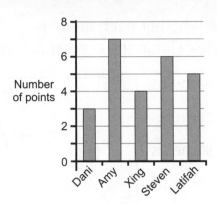

8. The bar chart shows the scores of five people in a spelling competition. They had to score 5 points or more to get to the next round of the competition. How many people got to the next round?

Answer: _____

9. Amir made a pictogram to show how many doughnuts his customers bought in an afternoon. How many doughnuts did Mr Blundell and Mrs Chong buy altogether? Circle the correct answer.

Mr Melton	◎ ◎
Mrs Chong	◎ ◎ ◎
Mrs Jones	◎ ◎ ◖
Mr Blundell	◎ ◖

◎ = 4 doughnuts

A   15   C   12   E   18
B   10   D   14

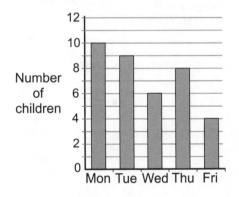

10. This bar chart shows the number of children who went to a windsurfing club on five days. How many more children went to the club on Tuesday than on Friday?

Answer: _____

11. Mrs Spriggs counted how many medals each team won on sports day. She made a bar chart to show the results. Circle the statement that is true.

A   Team 1 won 4 medals.

B   Team 2 won 3 medals.

C   Team 3 won the most medals.

D   11 medals were won in total.

E   Teams 1 and 2 won 8 medals in total.

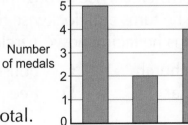

/ 4

Angles

Five angles are marked on the shape below. Decide whether each angle is smaller than, greater than or the same as a right angle. Circle the correct answer.

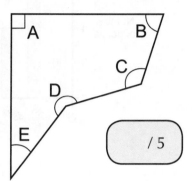

1.   Angle A: smaller than   greater than   the same as

2.   Angle B: smaller than   greater than   the same as

3.   Angle C: smaller than   greater than   the same as

4.   Angle D: smaller than   greater than   the same as

5.   Angle E: smaller than   greater than   the same as

/ 5

6.   How many right angles are there in a square?

Answer: _____

7.   Jane is facing north. She turns anticlockwise to face west.
     How many right angles does she turn through?

Answer: _____

Hint: Anticlockwise is the opposite direction to the way that clock hands move.

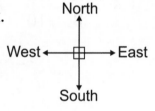

8.   Look at the angle on the right. Which of these statements is true?
     Circle the correct answer.

     A   It is smaller than one right angle.
     B   It is equal to one right angle.
     C   It is smaller than two right angles
     D   It is equal to two right angles.
     E   It is greater than two right angles.

9.   Simon is at X on the map. He is facing the church.
     He turns clockwise through five right angles.
     Then he turns anticlockwise through one right angle.
     What is he facing now? Circle the correct answer.

     A   church   **C**   house   **E**   bus
     B   car   **D**   tree

/ 4

2D Shapes

Circle 'True' or 'False' for each of these statements.

1. A triangle has 3 sides.   True   False

2. A hexagon has 5 sides.   True   False

3. An octagon has 8 sides.   True   False

4. A square has curved sides.   True   False

5. A rectangle is a quadrilateral.   True   False

 / 5

6. Poppy chooses a shape out of a bag and says, 'My shape has 4 right angles'. Which of these shapes did Poppy choose? Circle the correct answer.

   A   circle   **C**   pentagon   **E**   rectangle
   B   semi-circle   **D**   triangle

7. Which of these shapes is a pentagon? Circle the correct answer.

   A   **B**   **C**   **D**   **E**

8. Which of these shapes always has sides that are all the same length? Circle the correct answer.

   A   square   **C**   pentagon   **E**   rectangle
   B   octagon   **D**   triangle

9. Which of the following is the missing label from this Venn diagram? Circle the correct answer.

   A   3 sides
   B   3 corners
   C   No right angles
   D   At least 1 right angle
   E   4 corners

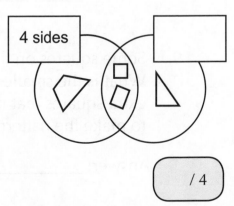

/ 4

Section Five — Shape and Space

Symmetry

Look at the letters in this word: **H E N**

1. Which of these letters has only one line of symmetry? Answer: _____

2. Which of these letters has two lines of symmetry?   Answer: _____

3. Which of these letters has no lines of symmetry?   Answer: _____

Tim uses a stencil to write this three-digit number:

4. Which of these digits has one line of symmetry?   Answer: _____

5. Which of these digits has two lines of symmetry?   Answer: _____

/ 5

6. Here is one half of a shape. The whole shape has one line of symmetry. Which of the shapes below could be the whole shape? Circle the correct answer.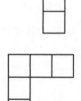

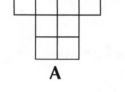   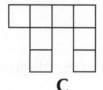

   A   **B**   **C**   **D**   **E**

7. This rectangle has one line of symmetry marked on it. Which of these diagrams shows its other line of symmetry? Circle the correct answer.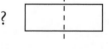

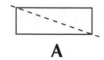   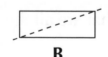   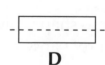   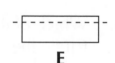

   A   **B**   **C**   **D**   **E**

8. How many lines of symmetry does this triangle have?

    Answer: _____

9. Some squares on this grid are shaded. What is the smallest number of extra squares that must be shaded to make the pattern symmetrical?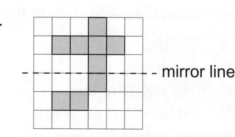

    — mirror line

    Answer: _____

/ 4

3D Shapes

Write the letter of the correct 3D shape next to its name.

1. cone   Answer: _____

2. cuboid   Answer: _____

3. hemisphere   Answer: _____

4. pyramid   Answer: _____

A   **B**   **C**   **D**

/ 4

5. How many faces does a cube have?   Answer: _____

6. Which of the following describes the faces of a cylinder?
   Circle the correct answer.

   A   2 curved faces and 1 flat face
   B   3 curved faces
   C   3 flat faces
   D   1 curved face and 2 flat faces
   E   3 flat faces and 1 curved face

7. How many of the shapes on the right are prisms?

   Answer: _____

   Hint: The two faces at the ends of a prism are exactly the same shape.

   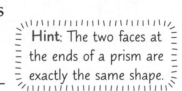

8. Ahmed is describing a shape. He says, 'Two of the faces are triangles'.
   Which type of shape could it be? Circle the correct answer.

   A   cylinder   **C**   triangular prism   **E**   cone
   B   sphere   **D**   cuboid

9. Look at the Venn diagram. Which of these shapes can go in place of X?
   Circle the correct answer.

   A   pyramid
   B   cube
   C   triangular prism
   D   cuboid
   E   cone

   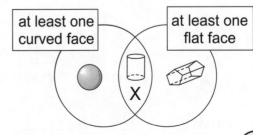

   at least one curved face   at least one flat face

   / 5

Shape Problems

Look at the shapes below and answer questions 1-4.

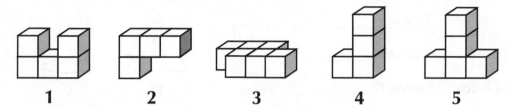

1   **2**   **3**   **4**   **5**

1. Which two shapes contain 4 cubes?   Answer: _____ and _____

2. Which two shapes contain 5 cubes?   Answer: _____ and _____

3. Which shape contains 6 cubes?   Answer: _____

4. Which shape would look like this if it was turned upside down?

                       Answer: _____

/ 4

5. Which of the shapes below is the same as the shape in the box? Circle the correct answer.

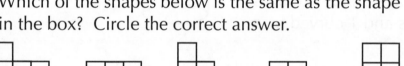

               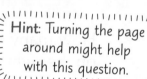

A   **B**   **C**   **D**   **E**

Hint: Turning the page around might help with this question.

6. Which of the diagrams below shows this cube from above? Circle the correct answer.

  A   **B**   **C**   **D**   **E**

7. Which two of the shapes below can be put together to make a pentagon?

    A   **B**   **C**   **D**   **E**

Answer: _____ and _____

/ 3

Coordinates

Look at this plan of a garden and answer questions 1-4.

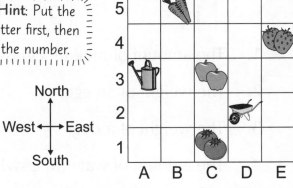

1. What square are the carrots in?

   Answer: _____

   Hint: Put the letter first, then the number.

2. What square are the strawberries in?

   Answer: _____

3. What square are the tomatoes in?

   Answer: _____

4. Which direction must you walk in to get from the apples to the tomatoes?   Answer: _____

/ 4

5.

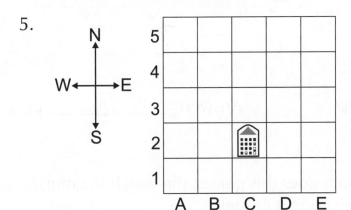

Harry has a toy that moves. The toy starts at square C2 and is facing north. The toy moves forward 3 squares. Which square does the toy move to?

Answer: _____

6. Which of these instructions lead from Sarah's house to the castle? Circle the correct answer.

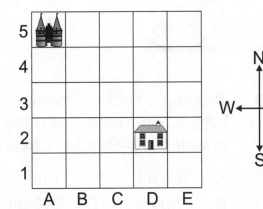

   A   north 3 squares, west 3 squares
   B   north 3 squares, west 2 squares
   C   west 3 squares, north 2 squares
   D   north 3 squares, east 3 squares
   E   east 2 squares, north 3 squares

7.

   The first letter of Jhara's secret word is in square A3. The second letter is in square C1, and the third is in square B2. What is his word? Circle the correct answer.

   A   BAT   C   TEN   E   TEA
   B   TAB   D   TAN

/ 3

Section Five — Shape and Space

Units

Which of these units would you use to measure the objects below?

| l | g | ml | kg |

1. The amount of milk in a glass.   Answer: _____

2. The weight of an egg.   Answer: _____

3. The weight of a dog.   Answer: _____

4. The amount of water in a swimming pool.   Answer: _____

/ 4

5. What temperature does this thermometer show? Circle the correct answer.

    A   30 °C   D   26 °C
    B   27 °C   E   28 °C
    C   25 °C

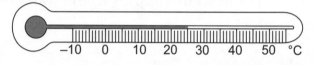

6. Jane's desk is 200 cm long.
    How long is the desk in metres?   Answer: _____ m

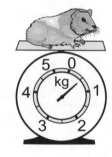

7. How much does this guinea pig weigh in grams?
    Circle the correct answer.

    A   25 g   C   500 g   E   5 g
    B   50 g   D   5000 g

    Hint: There are 1000 g in 1 kg.

8. This bottle holds 1 litre of water when it is full.
    Which of the following is the best estimate of the amount
    of water in the bottle? Circle the correct answer.

    A   500 ml   C   1 ml   E   200 ml
    B   750 ml   D   999 ml

9. Lucas has some sticky dots. They are each 5 mm wide.
    He sticks 10 dots in a line. How many centimetres long is the line?

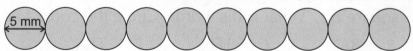

5 mm

    Answer: _____ cm

/ 5

Time

1. How many minutes are there in 1 hour?   Answer: _____

2. How many seconds are there in 1 minute?   Answer: _____

3. How many days are there in 1 week?   Answer: _____

4. How many hours are there in 1 day?   Answer: _____

5. How many months are there in 1 year?   Answer: _____   / 5

6. Elise and her friends do a 10 km race. The table shows how long it took them. Who won the race?

   Answer: _____

Elise	59 minutes
George	1 hour 6 minutes
Ali	56 minutes
Heather	1 hour 14 minutes
Hussein	1 hour 7 minutes

7. What time is shown on this clock? Circle the correct answer.

   A   20 minutes to 11   **D**   25 minutes to 11

   B   25 minutes past 10   **E**   25 minutes to 10

   C   20 minutes to 10

8. This is the timetable for Class 3D. One of the times is missing. Break lasts for 15 minutes. What time does Science start?

   Answer: _____ : _____

Activity	Start Time
Maths	9:00
PE	10:00
Break	10:45
Science	
Lunch	12:00

9. Lou finishes school at ten minutes past three. Football club starts at half past three. How long must Lou wait from the end of school until the start of football club?

   Answer: _____ minutes

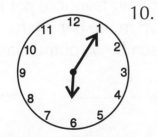

10. What time comes 45 minutes before the time shown on this clock? Circle the correct answer.

    A   15 minutes past 5   **D**   20 minutes past 4

    B   25 minutes past 5   **E**   20 minutes past 5

    C   20 minutes past 6   / 5

Section Six — Units and Measures

Mixed Problems

1. A merry-go-round turns three times each minute.
    How many times does it turn in one hour?   Answer: _____

2. Yusef buys one cake and one drink.
    How much does this cost to the nearest pound?

    Answer: £ _____

    PRICE LIST
    Sandwiches £2.30 each
    Cakes   £1.60 each
    Drinks   80p each

3. It takes Russell 6 minutes to iron a shirt. He has 5 shirts to iron.
    He starts ironing at half past 4. What time will he finish ironing?
    Circle the correct answer.

    A   5 minutes to 5   C   Half past 5   E   5 o'clock
    B   5 minutes past 5   D   Ten minutes past 5

4. Mika drew the lines shown and reflected them in the mirror
    line to make a shape. Circle the name of the shape.

    A   quadrilateral   C   rectangle   E   hexagon
    B   pentagon   D   octagon

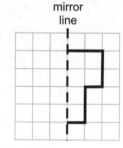
mirror line

5. 50 cm of ribbon costs 20p.
    How much will it cost to buy 3 m of ribbon?

    Answer: £ _____

    Hint: There are 100 cm in 1 m.

6. Which number below could go in the shaded part
    of the Venn diagram? Circle the correct answer.

    A 9   B 12   C 6   D 8   E 5

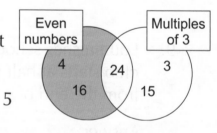
Even numbers   Multiples of 3
4   24   3
16   15

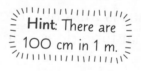

7. There are 32 children in Class 3E. They
    were all asked what their favourite pet is.
    The results are shown in the bar chart.
    Which pet was chosen by $1/4$ of the class?

    Answer: _____

Number of Children

12
10
8
6
4
2
0
Dog   Cat   Spider   Rabbit   Rat
Favourite Pet

/ 7

Assessment Test 1

The rest of the book contains six assessment tests to help you
improve your maths skills. Allow 30 minutes to do this test.
Work as quickly and as carefully as you can.

If you want to attempt each test more than once, you will need to print
multiple-choice answer sheets for these questions from our website
— go to cgpbooks.co.uk/11plus/answer-sheets. If you'd prefer to answer them
in standard write-in format, either write your answers in the spaces provided or
circle the **correct answer** from the options **A** to **E**.

1. Which of these numbers has the lowest value?

    A 255   **B** 201   **C** 270   **D** 249   **E** 210

2. Samuel read twelve books during the week and nine at the weekend.

    How many books did Samuel read altogether?

    Answer: _____

3. Which of these shapes is a cuboid?

    A   **B**   **C**   **D**   **E**

4. 24 cards are shared equally between 3 people.

    How many cards does each person get?

    Answer: _____

5. Look at the map on the right.

    What is in square C2?

    A swing   **C** tree   **E** chickens

    B slide   **D** sheep

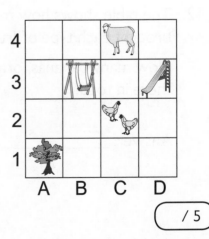

/ 5

Carry on to the next question → →

6. How many of the numbers in the box are multiples of 10?

| 90 | 53 | 10 | 21 | 5 |

  A 1   **B** 2   **C** 3   **D** 4   **E** 5

7. What is the missing number in this calculation?

    ☐ ÷ 6 = 8   Answer: _____

8. What number is 30 more than 273?   Answer: _____

9. Which of these clocks shows the time as 10 minutes to 7?

   A   **B**   **C**   **D**   **E**

10. There are 380 chairs in the school hall.
They are arranged in 10 equal rows.

How many chairs are there in each row?   Answer: _____

11. Which of these is the most likely weight of a £1 coin?

  A 500 g   **B** 10 kg   **C** 1000 g   **D** 1 kg   **E** 10 g

12. The table shows how many children in Year 3 brought each type of fruit to school.

How many bananas, oranges and peaches were there in total?

Answer: _____

Fruit	Number of children
Apple	12
Orange	10
Banana	9
Pear	7
Peach	8

/ 7

13. Find the difference between 248 and 36.   Answer: _____

14. What fraction of this rectangle is shaded?

    A ³⁄₄   **C** ¹⁄₄   **E** ⁵⁄₆

    B ¹⁄₆   **D** ⁴⁄₅

15. Paul spends 4 minutes in total brushing his teeth each day.

    How many minutes does he spend brushing his teeth in one week?

    A   40 minutes   **C**   28 minutes   **E**   7 minutes

    B   24 minutes   **D**   20 minutes

16. How many lines of symmetry does this shape have?

    Answer: _____

17. George looked at the colour of the cars in a car park.
    He made this pictogram of his results.

    How many silver cars were there?

    A 8   **C** 16   **E** 12
    B 14   **D** 3¹⁄₂

18. Louisa's knitting is 46 cm long.
    Tony's knitting is twice as long.

    How long is Tony's knitting?   Answer: _____ cm

19. Dotun counts on from 3 in steps of 8.

    Which of these numbers does he count?

    A 36   **B** 33   **C** 39   **D** 27   **E** 25

/ 7

Carry on to the next question → →

Assessment Test 1

20. A field is 138 m long.

What is this length rounded to the nearest 10 m? Answer: _____ m

21. Which of these shapes is not a hexagon?

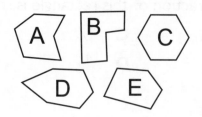

Answer: _____

22. 5 more children in Class 3 bring a packed lunch than have school dinners.

Which bar chart below shows this?

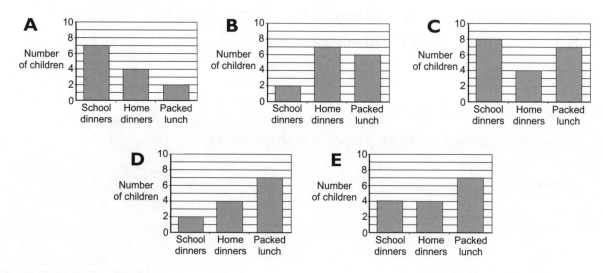

23. Simon and Ahmed go to the funfair. They go on 3 rides each.

How much do they spend in total?

A £8 **C** £24 **E** £25

B £12 **D** £14

24. Raisins cost 15p for every 100 g.
How much will 1 kg of raisins cost?

A £1.50 **B** £15 **C** £10 **D** £3 **E** £6

25. John has these values of coins.
He buys a drink for 89p.

£1 50p 10p 5p 2p

How much money does he have left?

A 67p **B** 68p **C** 88p **D** 78p **E** 79p

/ 6

End of Test

Assessment Test 2

Allow 30 minutes to do this test. Work as quickly and as carefully as you can.

You can print **multiple-choice answer sheets** for these questions from our website — go to <u>cgpbooks.co.uk/11plus/answer-sheets</u>. If you'd prefer to answer them in standard write-in format, either write your answers in the spaces provided or circle the **correct answer** from the options **A** to **E**.

1.   What is 8 multiplied by 100?   Answer: _____

2.   Write the number five hundred and seven in digits.

     Answer: _____

3.   How many right angles are there in this shape?
     A   0   **C**   2   **E**   4
     B   3   **D**   1

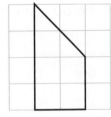

4.   Max keeps his toy cars in three boxes.
     There are nine cars in each box.

     How many toy cars does Max have in total?   Answer: _____

5.   Which of the following is the best unit to use to measure the length of a book?
     A   g   **B**   m   **C**   cm   **D**   km   **E**   ml

6.   Sarah has 42 yellow counters and 19 blue counters.

     How many counters has she got in total?

     Answer: _____

7.   Look at this sequence: 5, 8, 11, 14

     What is the next number in the sequence?

     Answer: _____

/ 7

Carry on to the next question → →

8. How many lines of symmetry does this shape have?

   Answer: _____

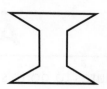

9. Jamal is drawing this pictogram to show the colours of the roses in his garden.

   There are 9 white roses. How many symbols should Jamal use to show this?

   A 9   **C** 4   **E** 3½
   B 18   **D** 4½

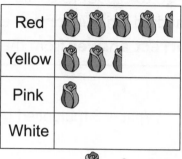

= 2 roses

10. There are 160 boys in a school. Half of them wear gloves.

    How many of the boys wear gloves?

    Answer: _____

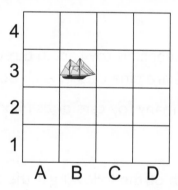

11. Which square is the ship in?

    A B2   **C** B3   **E** B1
    B A3   **D** C1

12. What is the name of this shape?

    A triangle   **C** rectangle   **E** octagon
    B pentagon   **D** hexagon

13. What fraction of this spinner is spotty?

    A ³⁄₄   **C** ²⁄₆   **E** ³⁄₆
    B ²⁄₅   **D** ³⁄₅

/ 6

14. What is the name of the 3D shape on the right?

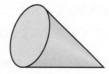

    A cube   **C** cylinder   **E** sphere

    B cuboid   **D** cone

15. Which of the following calculations has the biggest answer?

    A 60 ÷ 10   **C** 15 ÷ 3   **E** 14 ÷ 2

    B 40 ÷ 10   **D** 40 ÷ 5

16. Norbert's clock is shown on the right. It is 5 minutes fast. What is the correct time?

    A 20 minutes past 8   **D** 5 minutes to 8

    B 5 minutes past 8   **E** 10 minutes to 8

    C 10 minutes past 8

17. Which of the following numbers goes in the shaded part of the Venn diagram?

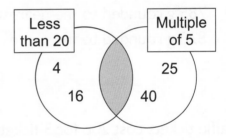

    A 15   **C** 34   **E** 7

    B 30   **D** 8

18. Tony, Arif, Susan and Ben play a computer game. The table shows how long it took each of them to complete a level.

    How many seconds faster was Arif than Ben?

    Answer: _____ seconds

Name	Time
Tony	54 seconds
Arif	27 seconds
Susan	42 seconds
Ben	1 minute

19. Sunita asked some people whether they liked strawberry, chocolate or vanilla ice cream best.

    Her results are shown in the bar chart.

    How many people did Sunita ask altogether?

    Answer: _____

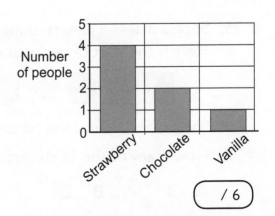

/ 6

Carry on to the next question → →

20. Holly has 70 stickers. She sticks 22 of them on her wall,
5 of them on her maths book and the rest on her bike.

How many stickers does she stick on her bike?   Answer: _____

21. Jasmine needs 875 ml of vinegar.
She measures the vinegar that she has in a jug.
How much more vinegar does she need?

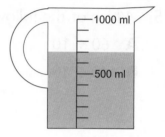

A	275 ml	**C**	175 ml	**E**	805 ml
B	200 ml	**D**	375 ml		

22. Which of these is 800 g?

A 890 g rounded to the nearest 100 g
B 775 g rounded to the nearest 10 g
C 815 g rounded to the nearest 10 g
D 785 g rounded to the nearest 10 g
E 820 g rounded to the nearest 100 g

23. Raffle tickets cost 20p for 3 tickets. There are 30 children in Mrs Brown's class.
How much does it cost Mrs Brown to buy a ticket for each child in her class?

A £2   **B** £6   **C** £5   **D** £10   **E** £3

24. What is 354 + 136?   Answer: _____

25. Sophia makes a pattern using four different shapes.
Here is the start of her pattern.

She carries on until the pattern contains 16 shapes.

How many of the 16 shapes are circles?

A 8   **B** 2   **C** 4   **D** 5   **E** 6   (/ 6)

End of Test

Assessment Test 3

Allow 30 minutes to do this test. Work as quickly and as carefully as you can.

You can print **multiple-choice answer sheets** for these questions from our website — go to cgpbooks.co.uk/11plus/answer-sheets. If you'd prefer to answer them in standard write-in format, either write your answers in the spaces provided or circle the **correct answer** from the options **A** to **E**.

1. What number is 40 less than 68?   Answer: _____

2. What is the biggest number you can make using these three cards? You can only use each card once.

   Answer: _____

3. What shape is a tennis ball?
   A cube   **C** cylinder   **E** sphere
   B cuboid   **D** cone

4. Latif gets 13 questions correct in a test.
   Amy gets double this number correct.

   How many questions did Amy get correct?   Answer: _____

5. What value is the arrow pointing to on this number line?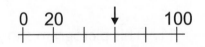

   Answer: _____

6. Gemma's birthday party is at quarter to six.

   Which clock shows this time?

   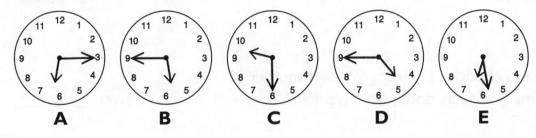

7. Paul has 16 pencils. ¼ of them are blunt.

How many of his pencils are blunt?   Answer: _____

8. What is the next number in this sequence?

962, 862, 762, 662...

A 652   **B** 462   **C** 562   **D** 661   **E** 552

9. Tina has 730 photos. She shares them equally between 10 albums.

How many photos does she put in each album?

Answer: _____

10. Which of these instructions lead from the tent to the campfire?

A south 3 squares, east 3 squares
B south 1 square, west 3 squares
C south 1 square, east 3 squares
D east 2 squares, south 1 square
E east 3 squares, north 1 square

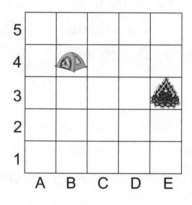

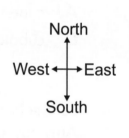

11. This pictogram shows the different types of pizza that a group of people ate on their holiday to Italy.

How many ham pizzas and chicken pizzas did they eat in total?

Answer: _____

Cheese	🍕 🍕 🍕 🍕
Ham	🍕 🍕 🍕
Mushroom	🍕
Chicken	🍕 🍕

🍕 = 2 pizzas

12. Juan has 126 stickers. Greg gives him another 33.
How many stickers does Juan have now?   Answer: _____

/ 6

13. A spider crawls up four bricks in a wall.
Each brick is 6 cm high.

How far does the spider crawl in total?

Answer: _____ cm

14. Barack shoots four paintballs at this target. His total score
is found by adding up the points for each paintball.

What is his total score?

A 22   **C** 26   **E** 30
B 24   **D** 28

15. How many centimetres are there in 4 metres?   Answer: _____ cm

16. What is the difference between 299 and 401?

A 2   **B** 102   **C** 101   **D** 202   **E** 302

17. Which of the shapes below has exactly three right angles?

    A   **B**   **C**   **D**   **E**

18. How many lines of symmetry are there in this shape?

Answer: _____

19. 20 children voted whether to grow carrots or peas
in the school garden. The number of children who
voted for carrots is shown on the bar chart.
The bar for peas has not yet been drawn.

How many children voted for peas?

A 17   **C** 16   **E** 20
B 15   **D** 12

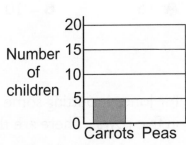

/ 7

Carry on to the next question → →

Assessment Test 3

20. Mrs Smith buys three T-shirts. Each T-shirt costs £9.
    How much change does she get from £40?   Answer: £ _____

21. This table shows how long five children
    spent on their homework.

    Which child's time is 50 minutes when
    rounded to the nearest 10 minutes?

    Answer: _____

Abdul	44 minutes
Bilal	45 minutes
Claire	55 minutes
David	58 minutes
Elliot	42 minutes

22. The Singh family are going on holiday. Their suitcases weigh 17 kg and 25 kg.
    They are only allowed to take 40 kg of luggage in total on the plane.

    How many kilograms of extra luggage do they have?

    A 2 kg   **B** 3 kg   **C** 8 kg   **D** 12 kg   **E** 5 kg

23. Which of these shapes will go in the
    shaded area of the sorting diagram?

    A   **B**   **C**   **D**   **E**

	Black	White
Straight sides only	◣ ⬟	⬡ ▢
At least one curved side		⬖ ◯

24. It takes Brian 30 minutes to bake a cake in his oven.
    He can only bake one cake at a time.

    How many cakes can he bake in two and a half hours?

    A 5   **B** 10   **C** 2   **D** 4   **E** 3

25. Mr Jones is putting some paintings on the classroom wall. He puts the paintings
    in five rows. There are the same number of paintings in each row.

    Which of the following could be the total number of paintings that he puts up?

    A 12   **B** 13   **C** 19   **D** 15   **E** 22   / 6

End of Test

Assessment Test 4

Allow 30 minutes to do this test. Work as quickly and as carefully as you can.

You can print **multiple-choice answer sheets** for these questions from our website — go to cgpbooks.co.uk/11plus/answer-sheets. If you'd prefer to answer them in standard write-in format, either write your answers in the spaces provided or circle the **correct answer** from the options **A** to **E**.

1. What number is the arrow pointing to on the number line below?

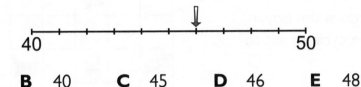

A 56   **B** 40   **C** 45   **D** 46   **E** 48

2. What is 65 × 10?   Answer: _____

3. Mrs Platt sells 5 different boxes of chocolates. The table shows how many chocolates are in each box.

    Which box contains the most chocolates?

    Answer: _____

	Number of chocolates
Box 1	29
Box 2	21
Box 3	17
Box 4	8
Box 5	28

4. How many cubes are there in this model?

    Answer: _____

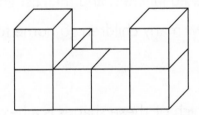

5. Jenny wants to measure the length of her cat. What unit of measurement should she use?

    A millilitres   **C** metres   **E** kilograms
    B centimetres   **D** kilometres

6. What is 55 rounded to the nearest ten?

    Answer: _____

/ 6

Carry on to the next question → →

7. Which of these numbers has the lowest value?

   A 128   **B** 131   **C** 182   **D** 126   **E** 201

8. Jack's puppies weigh 4 kg, 12 kg and 8 kg.

   How much do they weigh altogether?   Answer: _____ kg

9. Look at the grid on the right.

   In what direction does the boy in
   the centre need to cycle to get to
   the dog?

   Answer: _____

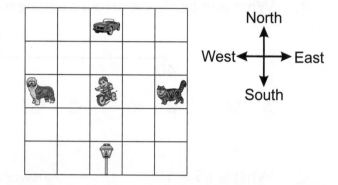

10. Choose the correct number to continue this sequence:

    1,   7,   13,   19,   _____ ...

    A 20   **B** 25   **C** 21   **D** 15   **E** 31

11. There are 32 children in Class B. At lunchtime,
    17 children have hot dinners, 12 children bring
    packed lunches, and the rest go home for lunch.

    How many children go home for lunch?   Answer: _____

12. Which of these shapes is a hexagon?

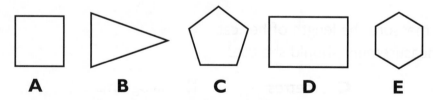

       A   **B**   **C**   **D**   **E**

13. What will be the total cost of five pencils costing 49p each?

    A £2.50   **C** £2.55   **E** £2.45
    B £2.40   **D** £2.49

/ 7

14. Marcus shares a bag of 54 sweets equally between himself and 5 friends.
How many sweets will each person get?

Answer: _____

15. The numbers of goals scored by members of the school
football team are shown in the pictogram.

How many more goals did David score than Heather?

Answer: _____

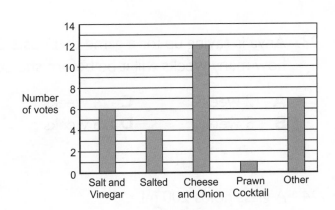

= 4 goals

16. Dani normally pays £15 for a horse-riding lesson.
On Tuesday there is $\frac{1}{3}$ off the price of each lesson.

How much money does Dani save on Tuesday?   Answer: £ _____

17. Mrs Dawes buys a burger meal for £2.99 and a child's meal for £1.99.
How much will the food cost her altogether?

Answer: £ _____

18. The children in Class 4 voted for
their favourite flavour of crisps.

How many more children voted
for cheese and onion than
prawn cocktail?

Answer: _____

19. The Ahmed family are going on two flights. Their first flight will take
50 minutes, and their second flight will take 4 hours and 40 minutes.

How long will the two flights take in total?

A   5 hours and 30 minutes   D   5 hours and 90 minutes
B   5 hours and 40 minutes   E   4 hours and 50 minutes
C   5 hours and 50 minutes

/ 6

Carry on to the next question → →

Assessment Test 4

20. Which set of numbers can be put in the empty box in the sorting diagram?

	odd	even
multiple of 7	7 21 35	
not a multiple of 7	1 25 37	26 50 82

A   14 and 24   **D**   13 and 42
B   14 and 28   **E**   21 and 30
C   14 and 46

21. Fran spends five days at school each week. She gets a bus to school and another bus home again. Each bus ride costs £1.20.

How much does she spend on bus fares altogether in a week?

A   £5   **D**   £12
B   £6   **E**   £24
C   £11

22. Which two 3D shapes below have the same number of faces?

1   **2**   **3**   **4**   **5**

A   3 and 5   **C**   1 and 5   **E**   4 and 5
B   1 and 3   **D**   2 and 4

23. Anya is saving up for a game that costs £3.00. If she saves 50p each week, how many weeks will it be before she can buy the game?

A   2 weeks   **C**   4 weeks   **E**   6 weeks
B   3 weeks   **D**   5 weeks

24. A glass holds 200 ml.

How many glasses of juice can be filled
from a jug holding 5 litres of juice?   Answer: _____

25. Danesh is hiring a hall for a party. The cost of the hall is £25, plus £5 for each of the 12 friends he has invited.

What is the total cost of the hall?

A   £37   **B**   £40   **C**   £60   **D**   £85   **E**   £100

/ 6

End of Test

Assessment Test 5

Allow 30 minutes to do this test. Work as quickly and as carefully as you can.

You can print **multiple-choice answer sheets** for these questions from our website — go to cgpbooks.co.uk/11plus/answer-sheets. If you'd prefer to answer them in standard write-in format, either write your answers in the spaces provided or circle the **correct answer** from the options **A** to **E**.

Name	Time Taken (seconds)
Cary	23
Jo	19
Mika	26
Leah	21
Zara	24

1. The table shows the results of an egg and spoon race.

    Who finished the race in the shortest time?

    A Cary   **C** Mika   **E** Zara
    B Jo   **D** Leah

2. What is 6 × 9?

    A 45   **C** 56   **E** 60
    B 52   **D** 54

3. Tina used four identical tiles to make the shape on the right.

    What shape are the tiles that she used?

    A rectangles   **D** hexagons
    B pentagons   **E** squares
    C triangles

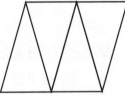

4. Mr Kean splits his class into teams of four for a quiz.
    There are 28 children in the class. How many teams will there be?

    Answer: _____

5. An ice cream seller made this pictogram of the number of ice creams he sold over five days.

    How many ice creams did he sell on Tuesday and Wednesday in total?

    Answer: _____

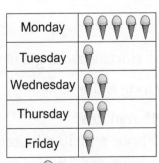

= 5 ice creams

/ 5

Carry on to the next question → →

6. Luka counts back in steps of 4 from 40.

   Which of these numbers will he not count?

   A 29   **B** 32   **C** 24   **D** 36   **E** 20

7. Peter is 165 cm tall. Kat is 98 cm tall.
   What is the difference between their heights?   Answer: _____ cm

8. Simon starts from his house in square C3.
   He walks 1 square south and 2 squares west.

   Which square does he get to?

   A E2   **C** A4   **E** A2
   B B4   **D** B1

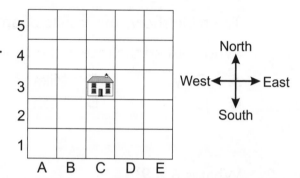

9. A grandmother shares £250 equally between her 10 grandchildren.

   How much money does each grandchild get?

   Answer: £ _____

10. Which of the following does not equal 30?
    A ½ of 60   **C** 22 + 8   **E** 10 × 3
    B 5 × 6   **D** 80 − 40

11. Which of these letters has no lines of symmetry?

    O D U H S

    Answer: _____

12. Abbas starts watching a film at 5:15 pm. The film finishes at 6:30 pm.

    How long is the film?

    A 45 minutes   **D** 1 hour and 45 minutes
    B 1 hour and 30 minutes **E** 2 hours and 15 minutes
    C 1 hour and 15 minutes

/ 7

13. Penny has saved £12. Her brother has saved four times as much.

How much money has Penny's brother saved?

Answer: £ _____

14. Ben buys a sandwich and pays with a £10 note.

How much change does he get?

A £5.01   C £5.11   E £4.11

B £6.01   D £6.11

Price List	
Sandwiches	£4.89
Chips	£3.85
Cakes	£2.99

15. Arun has a 3D shape with 5 faces. Which of these shapes could it be?

A cuboid   C cylinder   E triangular prism

B sphere   D cube

16. On Saturday Mr Green sold 8 kg of turnips, 21 kg of potatoes, 3 kg of carrots and 4 kg of onions.

What is the total weight of the vegetables he sold?   Answer: _____ kg

17. Which of these numbers should be put in the shaded section of the Venn diagram?

A 36   C 45   E 56

B 23   D 24

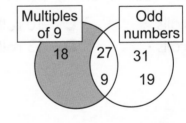

18. One bus passes Mrs Jones's house every 15 minutes, starting at 8 am.

How many buses will pass her house between 7:55 am and 9:05 am?

A 2   B 3   C 4   D 5   E 6

19. Which of the following equals 360?

A 359 rounded to the nearest 100   D 357 rounded to the nearest 10

B 36 rounded to the nearest 10   E 365 rounded to the nearest 10

C 340 rounded to the nearest 100

/ 7

Carry on to the next question → →

Assessment Test 5

20. Abbie buys a sofa at half price. If the full price of the sofa was £700, how much did Abbie pay?

Answer: £ _____

21. Luigi's restaurant ordered 5 packs of tomatoes on Friday and 10 packs on Saturday. Each pack contains 6 tomatoes. How many tomatoes did they order in total?

Answer: _____

22. The children in a swimming club are split into different age groups. The number of children in each group is shown on this bar chart.

Two new 11-year-olds join the club. How many children are in the 10-12 age group now?

Answer: _____

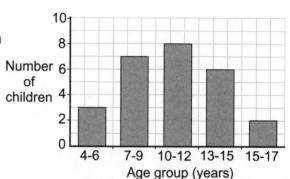

23. Meera needs 45 m of fencing to go around her garden. The fencing comes in rolls of 4 metres.

How many rolls of fencing does Meera need to buy?

A   11 rolls   C   10 rolls   E   15 rolls
B   12 rolls   D   13 rolls

24. This table shows the number of books read by members of a library over a month.

How many members read more than 15 books?

A   4   C   15   E   12
B   8   D   7

Number of books read	Number of members
0-5	8
6-10	12
11-15	7
16-20	4
More than 20	4

25. A jug of juice is shown on the right.

How many 250 ml cups can be filled from this jug?

Answer: _____

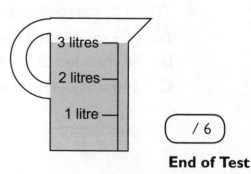

/ 6

End of Test

Assessment Test 6

Allow 30 minutes to do this test. Work as quickly and as carefully as you can.

You can print **multiple-choice answer sheets** for these questions from our website — go to cgpbooks.co.uk/11plus/answer-sheets. If you'd prefer to answer them in standard write-in format, either write your answers in the spaces provided or circle the **correct answer** from the options **A** to **E**.

1. What number is the arrow pointing to on this number line?

    Answer: _____

2. What is 165 – 55?   Answer: _____

3. What is 846 litres rounded to the nearest 100 litres?   Answer: _____ l

4. There are 6 eggs in one box.

    How many eggs will there be in 8 boxes?   Answer: _____

5. Peter has collected £2.50 for a sponsored run.
    His dad gives him an extra £3.30.

    How much money has Peter raised in total?

    A £5.80   **B** £4.90   **C** £7.10   **D** £6.30   **E** £6.50

6. Which of these shapes contains the most cubes?

    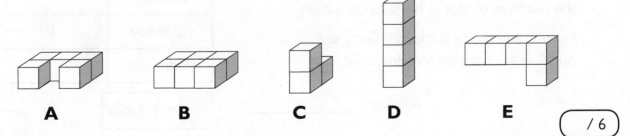

    A   **B**   **C**   **D**   **E**

    / 6

Carry on to the next question → →

7. Yanisa has seventeen £10 notes.

    How much money does she have in total?   Answer: £ _____

8. This table shows the ages of five children.

    Which two children have an age difference of 5 years?

    A Louisa and Ollie   **D** James and Sara

    B Jonah and Sara   **E** Louisa and James

    C Ollie and Jonah

Name	Age in years
Ollie	8
Jonah	4
Sara	1
James	6
Louisa	12

9. Which of these statements is true?

    A $9 < 6$ **C** $17 > 18$ **E** $14 > 11$

    B $10 > 20$ **D** $12 < 2$

10. What time is shown on this digital clock?

    A 15 minutes past 8   **D** 15 minutes to 8

    B Forty-five minutes past 9 **E** 20 minutes to 9

    C 15 minutes to 9

11. Which shape will go into the
    shaded box of the sorting table?

    A rectangle   **D** pentagon

    B cube   **E** sphere

    C triangle

	2D	3D
Square faces		
No square faces		

12. Gary counts the number of ducks in his
    garden pond. He makes a pictogram to show
    the number of ducks he sees on 3 days.

    How many more ducks did Gary see
    on Monday than on Wednesday?

    Answer: _____

Day	Number of ducks
Monday	▪ ▪ ▪
Tuesday	▪ ▪
Wednesday	▪

▪ = 4 ducks

/ 6

13. What fraction of this shape is shaded?

    A ⅛   **C** ¼   **E** ⅙

    B ⅓   **D** ½

14. There are 56 crayons in 7 packs.
    How many crayons are there in each pack?   Answer: _____

15. This table shows the results for Hartley Netball Club over three seasons.

    How many games did the team lose or draw in Season 3?

    Answer: _____

	Games Won	Games Drawn	Games Lost
Season 1	19	8	11
Season 2	16	10	12
Season 3	13	14	11

16. Millie makes a number sequence.
    She starts at 30 and adds on 6 each time.

    Which of these numbers will not be in her sequence?

    A 36   **B** 46   **C** 54   **D** 60   **E** 42

17. Three toffees and one pack of fruit chews cost 50p altogether. Each toffee costs 10p.

    How much is one pack of fruit chews?   Answer: _____ p

18. Which number is in the wrong section of the Venn diagram?

    A 28   **C** 15   **E** 40

    B 45   **D** 20

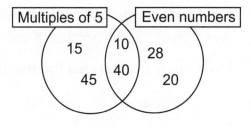

19. Shiloh is paid £8 for every 2 hours that he works.
    Shiloh earned £32 in March.

    How many hours did Shiloh work during March?

    A 6   **B** 4   **C** 8   **D** 2   **E** 10   / 7

20. This is the plan of a theme park.

   Ali starts at square B1. He walks
   3 squares north and 1 square east.

   Where does he end up?

   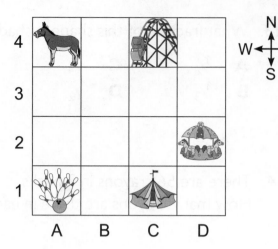

   A A4 — donkey ride
   B A1 — bowling alley
   C C1 — circus tent
   D D2 — merry-go-round
   E C4 — roller coaster

21. Marjorie halved a bag of 12 chocolate coins between
   Oscar and Ruby. Ruby ate half of her share.

   How many chocolate coins did Ruby have left?

   A 4   **B** 6   **C** 3   **D** 2   **E** 5

22. How many lines of symmetry does this shape have?

   Answer: _____

   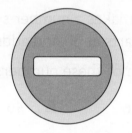

23. Mrs Bunn uses 1 kg of flour to make 100 cookies.

   How many grams of flour does she need to make one cookie?

   A 100 g   **B** 1 g   **C** 1000 g   **D** 50 g   **E** 10 g

24. One crate holds 8 bottles of milk.
   A milkman has 60 bottles of milk.

   How many crates does the milkman need?   Answer: _____

25. There are 29 children in Aimee's class.
   Aimee started making a bar chart to show
   how each child travels to school, but she
   hasn't drawn the last bar.

   How many children come by bus?

   Answer: _____

   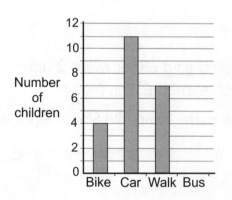

M3QE2

/ 6

End of Test